Contents

A Peaceful Place

As I sit in a peaceful place
I have a warm smile on my face

Nature is everywhere, all around
And it's here just waiting to be found

The distant sound of a river rushing
Wind through the leaves gently brushing

Birds flying with intent overhead
I lay down looking up just like in bed

A Sea of blue and clouds passing over
Chalky white like the cliffs of Dover

The sun's warmth shines deep and down
Helping to remove even my deepest frown

My body relaxes, my spirit strong
I hear the sounds of distant birdsong

Never again will I ever fear
As at this very moment, it is very clear

This is where the mind seeks its peace
Stillness prevails and restlessness will cease

My Friend Marion

Marion has been a good friend of mine
It's her birthday today, Aquarius is her sign
First, we met through our friend Mike
He has Enzo, she had Spike

Many memories we have shared
Her time for chats never spared
Often cooking and being the host
Providing food and games she can boast

Old Pottery Kiln we meet for lunch
Opens at 12 so too late for brunch
And Inner Space we have shared
Spiritual wellbeing, we both cared

A maker of jewellery to behold in wonder
The finished article is never a blunder
The gems, jewels and stones used too
In many colours from red to blue

Once a Manager in Human Resource
She's now in IT as a help desk source
A wife, a mother and nanny to two
Marion is there through and through

Giving her time to help family and friends
Support both virtual and real she sends
Have a birthday; happy and fun
Here are good wishes - approximately a ton

Covid 19 you are not welcome here

Covid 19 you are not welcome here
You're causing concern, worry and fear
Leave us alone and go elsewhere
Preferably another planet, we don't care

Just go, disappear; leave us alone
A curve ball it's true you have certainly thrown
Panic buying and empty shelves
Some people thinking only of themselves

A run on toilet rolls started fast
No normal shopping, we are completely aghast
With hand sanitizing gel all the rage
And you, the virus, taking centre stage

Shut are cafes, restaurants and bars
Who do you think you are to mimic SARS
Country by country the Government's plan
It's an invisible war, doing all they can

But the virus spreads silently and not seen
None of us can know where it has been
We have to help, all do our bit
And find new ways to keep ourselves fit

Physically, emotionally and mentally too
We will fight this virus like a military coup
The wonders of social media and mobile phones
Telling people to stay inside by using drones

But through the doom and gloom are rays of light
People's care for others in full sight
And video clips make us smile
Covering the globe mile by mile

Social distancing and self-isolation
New ways of living are in creation
But like all good Brits we will get through
All we need is a biscuit and a brew

Snowflake

A snowflake falling through the air
In which direction it doesn't care

In the sky high above
As soft and gentle as a flying dove

Down it floats from left to right
Swirling around like the wind and a kite

Its crystal-like pattern delicate to the touch
Its whiteness gleaming just as much

And slowly it falls with no sound
Until, finally, it reaches the ground

But its life is short, soon to be gone
A distant memory of a childhood song

Old woman

There was an old woman who lived in a tent
Many letters we knew she sent
Camped in a field with a stream nearby
She always wore a shirt but never a tie

Been there years as far as I can remember
Definitely Autumn, I think a September
She had a small stove for cooking her food
And a small teapot in which she brewed

She was polite enough if you said hello
And had a happy face with cheeks to glow
A conversation she would often strike
Interesting and witty which lots of people seemed to like

She didn't have much but was happy to share
Apart from those who would stop and stare
She wasn't deaf; no need to shout
And pretty educated I don't doubt

She had a dog obedient and quiet
But far too fat, needed to be on a diet
Watching the birds and animals live
Bits of food she would often give

And every day she sat on a stool
A basic black biro her only tool
And when not writing she was reading a book
Or a needle and thread mending clothes she took

Some days she was seen down at the stream
Scrubbing her clothes as if in a dream
And there between two trees they would hang
Being pegged up neatly as she sang

But once per week she left her tent
Walked to the post office where money she spent
And first time ever the postman came
A letter in hand, to deliver his aim

There I saw it, a smile so big
She and her dog did a dance and a jig
Within a week the tent was no more
Just a space; the green grassy floor

But rumour has it she became hugely rich
And moved to a castle with a bridge and a ditch
For years I never saw her until one day
She was in the street giving money away

Autumn

A watery sun shines above the field
Golden harvests ready to yield
Bales of hay sit neatly in lines
Tied together with string and twines

Tractor engines revving for work
A fox in the hedge continues to lurk
Waking up early you notice the dew
Signs of Autumn are starting anew

Summer has gone and now shorter days
Yes, there is sun but with weaker rays
A gentle breeze on our faces
Cyclists in shorts on their races

Leaves once strong, green and lush
Lighten and weaken to a yellowy crush
And if not yellow a raspberry red
And then they fall, the leaves are dead

Bushes and trees laden with fruit
Stand to attention like a Sunday suit
Berries ripe, ready for the taking
An oven turned on soon to be baking

But it's not all tranquillity and misty mornings
A storm in the Atlantic is rapidly forming
Its likely path, moving east
Deepening fast; to be a windy beast

Gales, rain and flooded roads
Ponds no safe place for frogs and toads
More and more the cloudy, dull days
The dreams of the past summer we all crave

Little children playing conkers
To the onlooker it looks sort of bonkers
The longer nights develop and pass
No longer a need to cut the grass

Trees now bare of any greenery
The landscape we love a changing scenery
Autumn has arrived, it is here
The dark early night now all too clear

Happy Easter Sunday

Happy Easter Sunday to all my friends
Given the situation we're all at loose ends

So here is my poem to make you smile
Hey they aren't that bad; don't run a mile (lol)

We all know lockdown isn't much fun
Especially this year with all the Spring sun

But the Easter Bunny is here to say
Disappear Covid, nobody wants you so go away

Friendship

True friendship in life is a rare gift
With ups and downs it's occasionally adrift

But the strength within reveals devotion
As we explore together all kinds of emotion

Friendships are there through thick and thin
To some like a glass of favourite gin

They take a few knocks but never fall
This is how true friendships stay standing tall

But when it feels lost, lazy or depleted
It must find itself get through difficulties repeated

It's like a flower; a seed to start
With leaves and petals unfolding apart

And when the right food and water do sow
Our friendship appears and it does grow

True Friendship, a rare commodity not to be sold
It's so precious; a nougat of gold

Each one is different; individual and unique
Some friendships are like a top-class boutique

But when a friendship breaks the mould
It's something to treasure and behold

And finally, friends care when I am down
A smile to develop and relieve my frown

Going on holiday

The engines roared with all their might
And there we were on a two-hour flight
Perfume, watches and duty free
Next snacks with coffee, chocolate or tea

The magazine read in 10 minutes flat
In my seat I calmly sat
Then I felt the plane's slow descent
The weather was fine no turbulence to torment

Doors opened, we were in Spain
Through passport control and baggage reclaim
The sunshine bright walking on to the bus
So many tourists arriving, what a crush

At the hotel we got our key
The balcony it had a view to see
Across the way was a cool blue ocean
The waves lapping in almost slow motion

The room was clean tidy and ready to use
Away from Britain and the depressing news
We unpacked our cases and our bags
In the corner traditional Spanish mags

Change into a T shirt, flip flops and shorts
Into the street; shops, cafes and all sorts
Outside at a table with café con leche
We were relaxed and not in the least bit tetchy

Lunchtime arrived English or Spanish or something in between
Maybe just cake and coffee topped with cream
It was Spain so let's do paella
Delicious and tasty I think I will tell her

The waitress smiled and was pleased
We practiced our Spanish but were never teased
2 weeks stretched out before us
By day sunbathing and tours on a bus

As night approached it was time to shower
The resort lit up like Blackpool tower
And after eating it's the bars we head
There are many hours before we hit our bed

Clap for Carers

Clap for Carers was a beautiful thing
Saying thank you to so many, the help you bring
The clinical expertise, support and compassion
None of you providing it in any sort of ration

Stacking the shelves and delivery drivers
Volunteers, admin staff and supervisors
At 8 o'clock we were together to unite
A virus spreading, we will fight

So many clapped and cheered in appreciation
From cities to villages across the nation
You are heroes and heroines shining with light
In what, it's clear, is a very difficult fight

But perhaps when Covid is finally gone
You are rewarded appropriately not just with a song
But proper wages, resources and pride
You the heroes standing side by side

The Gym

Waking up to the sound of rain
Water droplets beading the pane
Dark and windy I head for the gym
Yes, it's cold but I want to stay trim

Through the doors, towel and bottle complete
The muscle blokes are in, I feel so petite
A warm up and stretch is needed first
Water at the ready to quench my thirst

Rowing machine and cross cable flies
I dream about meat and potato pies
Nope not allowed, can't be done
Not even room for the smallest sticky bun

Onto the treadmill, time to run
Its serious stuff, I don't do it for fun
Programme and button at the ready
I'm there waiting, legs kept steady

Laying on the bench, dumbbells in hand
I push up and down thinking sun and sand
Soon my holiday, flying to Spain
Cerveza and Paella away from the rain

Incline, distance, speed and more
Could this really be less of a chore?
In the mirror face turning red
Why oh why am I not still in bed

A healthy body and mind I manage
Time and exercise erode the damage
Vegetables and vitamins, C D and E
Complex carbs, they really are the key

Porridge, yogurt and cottage cheese
All provide protein, shakes to please
Blueberries, bananas and cherries too
Make for something red, tasty and new

Silent and rested I meditate
Monthly improvements I celebrate
Positive and confident is my thought
Fitness and health are being sought

Building muscle, losing fat
Last few crunches on the mat
Becoming lean is what I dream
In the mirror, there to be seen

After an hour I am done
And yes, ok it wasn't much fun
Back through the doors to the world outside
I head for my car, briefcase by my side

Lazing on the beach

Laying on my sunbed looking out to sea
Relaxing enjoyment is the key

With waves on the sand gently lapping
And children running, laughing and clapping

I watch and listen to the people
I read my book about a church and tall steeple

After an hour laying in the sun
I'm getting hot like a newly baked bun

Time to paddle, take a dip
And then I think return for a kip

Hot sand underneath slowly I tread
Careful of the jellyfish someone said

I reach the water cool and blue
One toe in and then another two

Soon both feet and up to my knees
It's not so hard, bit of a breeze

With a slight dive I am in
It's refreshing I begin to swim

After a few minutes it's absolute bliss
The summer sea; it's something I miss

Men, women and children swim and splash
And on a rock further out waves do crash

The sun beats down on my face and shoulders
Underneath pure sand no pebbles or boulders

Half an hour and I am done
Time to drink and eat a real currant bun

Ahh!! The sand is baking
Passing sandcastles in the making

At last my sunbed; On it I leap
All day it's mine, mine to keep

I'm hungry and thirsty so out comes the food
Someone near me is sunbathing in the nude

No matter it's my lunch I am after
And I eat to the distant sound of laughter

Full and replenished I lay down
Content and smiling; slowly turning brown

The minutes tick, tick away
The parasol with its shade it does sway

And like a chicken I roast and bake
I'm soon browning for heaven's sake

After several hours I head for my car
The sun is falling like a Russian tzar

My day of sun comes to a close
And once again another doze

Mother Nature has had enough

Mother Nature has had enough
She had decided; time to be tough
Carbon emissions keep going up
Just throwing away our plastic cups
Raging bush fires scorched the earth
Animals and insects running for all their worth

And glaciers melting shrinking swift and fast
Some already a thing of the past
With heatwaves and drought just getting worse
It's all our own doing creating a curse
Incessant rain caused floods and misery
The worst many had seen in living history

And hundreds of species fight to stay alive
Coral reefs now only just able to survive
We flew round the globe without a worry
Society to be sure in far too much of a hurry
Long gone are the days of a simple life
We are cutting up the planet like cake to a knife

And whilst Greta and others try to slow us down
Mother Nature looks at us with a scolding frown
If you can't sort yourselves out and care for the planet
Then I must impose it; no excuses, god dammit
And what better way to make you stop and think
An infectious virus taking hold before you blink

Stay at home, dump less carbon
Grow seasonal vegetables in your garden
People listen! Change your behaviour
Otherwise a vaccine will not be your saviour

My favourite dog

His black spots on the pure white background
Hefty and solid he weighs many a pound
Enzo is his name he knows it well
Call him and he won't dwell

Asleep on the sofa he dozes content
A snore and a snuffle don't prevent
Suddenly he's up, quick as a flash
On the floor in a dash

Wanting his walk or his dinner
At my side he's a real winner
A face full of pleasure
He is a bundle of moving treasure

Scatty and boisterous his eyes full of love
He lays under the bed snug as a glove
Then suddenly a scraping sound comes from underneath
A nose, a paw and now his white teeth

A head pokes out inquisitive and excited
Two front legs and body delighted
He's out and bounding round the room
Tail wagging and sweeping like a broom

It's walkies time he knows for sure
A shoe in his mouth he gives me a paw
Yes, that's my trainer thank you so much
His collar secure; tight to the touch

Settled in the car he is patient
As I drive to the woods old and ancient
10 minutes later we arrive
Parked and ready, will I survive?

Through the trees all green and leafy
I look at Enzo he's even more beefy
Then the clearing the grass awaits
But Enzo is thinking- where are my mates

The long grass beckons swaying in the wind
Turning his head to me as he grinned
He's off darting and running through the grass
All I can see is his black and white arse

What is that animal, is it a rabbit?
Enzo sees it and he's off trying to grab it
Poor animal looks startled but nothing to fear
My gorgeous Dalmatian is nowhere near

An hour late we are back in the car
Hungry and tired we drive off the tar
Once home it is drink and food
A plate for us both of course; otherwise it's rude

And then on the sofa Enzo climbs
He's knackered for sure but had a good time
And just like that he's asleep and rested
And for me – I got my patience tested

I love my dog; very dearly
Just wish he could see things a bit more clearly
Until he wakes, I can rest
I need a smaller dog; I joke and jest

My Hidden Secret

My hidden secret shared by me alone
Its strength and tightness weigh me down
I don't feel loved I never did
This situation I know I must rid
The strength within needs to come to the fore
Before my heart and soul is ripped out at the core

At the window sill a bird sits and sings
And then a cat appears, it suddenly springs
I shout "fly little bird fly"
It does to safety and then I cry
The tears in my eyes roll down my cheek
My life remains grey, cold and bleak

Feeling trapped; like a bird in a cage
I feel it inside, a strong inner rage
Do I leave or do I stay?
Inside my head I think and pray
And then one day the cage is open
A silent voice appears to be spoken

I know I have wings and want to fly
Away from anger, fright and my endless cry
The silence can be deafening waiting to break
The depths of anguish like a deep dark lake
But at the window shines through the light
I must confront my ongoing fright

I deserve more in life without constant fear
To stop shedding tear after tear
And at that moment, without thinking
I use the phone without even blinking
"Escape for women hello can I help"
"Yes please, I can't take anymore" I practically yelp

My sister, Karen

My sister Karen you are one of a kind
In many ways, a gem of a find

Fun and happy, thoughtful and wise
You're up there high; a brother's best prize

At times when I'm down, you show you are there
Putting aside your life to show me loving care

And when I was lost, searching through a thick wood
You gave me your hand whenever you could

When I experienced stormy, dark days
You've been a ray of sunshine in so many ways

Taking the time to listen and show concern
It brought us closer together; to develop and learn

Yes, you can be lively and noisy, make no mistake
But that's your charm, like thick sugary icing on a cake

You bring joy and happiness into the room
Sweeping negativity out quickly with a broom

We've enjoyed many good times over the years
Laughing so much there were sometimes flurries of tears

And although not seeing you as frequently as I would like
Whattsapp "voices" I look forward to, like chocolate and marmite

So how do I end, what do I send?
Perhaps thank you Karen, my sister, my friend

Our Summer Place

Finally, it arrives our summer place
Secretive and special with emotional space

Where we are us and meet together
Hoping it will last, ages and forever

And whether we are given sunshine or storm
We know we feel safe, happy and warm

Our arms reach out and we don't feel lonely
It feels natural and loving, I suppose very homely

With hearts set free from worries and cares
It's our special time and not theirs

And through our eyes shining bright
We recognise our feelings and know it is right

It knows no dark clouds and gloomy skies
The silver linings in abundance and the time it flies

Blessed with depth and heart felt love
It's like a graceful, gliding, peace offering dove

We are two people who just want to share
Precious memories and more, in essence to care

Our hopes, our dreams, all our love
That summer place shining on us from above

But does it continue, does it end
Will we be lovers or just each a friend

Depression

Awake in the morning tired and stressed
Ten more minutes before I get dressed
I love my bed, so warm and cosy
Everything outside, doesn't seem rosy

Life is for living, so much to offer
But why oh why can I not bother
I want to enjoy life all of the time
But I just can't and it seems such a crime

The pressure I put on myself has no bounds
And life seems empty with no sounds
I feel void, fed up, vague and detached
Me and life don't seem very matched

People everywhere laugh and smile
But for me, life, seems like a pile
Weighing me down, stopping me thinking
All I feel is an incredible sinking

At the bottom of the well I look up
The sky above like the bottom of a cup
Empty, stained with smudged looking particles
Maybe the answer is read some articles

There is no ladder and it seems no luck
The quilt and blankets I do tuck
For a minute I feel good then it's gone
I'm back to feeling life is no song

My emotions are mixed but never good
Not even improved by my favourite pud
I need to eat, I need to drink
But it's really hard when I feel on the brink

I look at my list of actions and goals
Simple and few if truth be told
Therapy says they should help
But I feel limp and soggy like seaweed and kelp

Even by midday I'm worn out and tired
My brain isn't working just seems cross wired
Slowly the day passes and my illness fades
I feel slightly better but still on my crusade

And then it's bedtime, to turn out the light
Tomorrow starts again and so does my plight
I tell myself to get up earlier
But that's like saying my hair will be curlier

It won't happen, it's too straight
And once again I feel trapped in my crate

Enzo and the storm

A morning of sunshine gave way to cloud
And it wasn't long before the wind howled

Enzo felt it coming; the thunder and lightning
He didn't like it much, his stomach started tightening

The wind picked up as the storm drew near
Enzo first sleeping, now very clear

He headed inside, he wanted to shelter
This storm, he knew, would be a belter

First came the thunder and oh the wind howled
Enzo didn't like it, watching he growled

A lightning flash and a drop of rain
Then a deep roar and splash on the pane

One drop, two drops then many more
Within minutes it started to pour

But Enzo was inside, away from the storm
He laid in his bed all comfy and warm

And whilst the storm flashed and roared
Enzo fell asleep, dreamed and snored

Mum

Thank you mum for being there
You always show how much you care

Through thick and thin, black and white
Your love is strong, continuous with might

Always available, steady as a rock
A guarantee, like the ticking of a clock

A boat on the ocean, a captain tasked
You provide a home of sanctuary, no questions asked

A place to rest and relax at ease
Your reassuring face like honey to bees

With coffee and biscuits and cups of tea
You remain at the helm always helping us be

But it's not just those, you offer with love
But a home of peace like a spiritual dove

To the best mum in the world, what can I say
I guess it has to be, Happy Mother's Day

Smile like a clown

If you're feeling down, smile like a clown
Act cheery and happy, and always calm down

Like boulders big on your shoulders
Happiness is there even if it just smoulders

Reduce the weight that keeps you so heavy
Meet friends or go to the pub for a bevvy

Be like moths attracted to the light
And don't let your worries be your plight

Break them, separate them one by one
Or pull them out like currants in a bun

Within us all is growth and strength
Like swimming, strive for the extra length

And see the good things that surround you in life
Your friends, family and yes even your wife

'Cos life is still for living in a difficult time
A hill, a mountain they are there for the climb

So, like that clown smile, feel warm like the Azores
A good life is for the taking and remember it's yours

The Brazilian

She came into my life through an app
Our conversation flowed like a tap
. Tall and dark with a beautiful smile
Her white teeth gleaming for a mile
Yes we were different, not much the same
Yet we complimented each other like an umbrella and rain

Her first experience took her by surprise
Hard to determine what did it comprise
The first kiss was gentle, short and sweet
She was vulnerable, nervous when our lips were to meet
This was certainly like no ordinary get together
But something I will treasure and remember forever

Perhaps I knew she wasn't that way
She certainly didn't know from day to day
But we loved each other's company, friendship and chat
I helped her get settled, into her flat
Finally we agreed we needed to split
It was hard and intense and difficult to admit

What we had, was beautiful and warm
So many facets, like a new dawn
Time moves on but she remains my friend
A very lovely woman, I can't contend
Perhaps what we had was a bit like treasure
Certainly, a person to give much pleasure

I'm sure our memories will always remain
Neither of us in any way ever to blame
A woman I acknowledge; I won't forget
And a place in my heart will always be set

New Artist

More time on her hands, what to do
Let me try doing something completely new
She thought a while and then some more
And then it came to her she was sure

The palette of paint when dad had died
I'm going to try painting she thought with pride
Where to start she wasn't sure
Look at google for techniques and more

And so she began, slowly at first
Brushing strokes gently, the paper immersed
And soon the painting began to take shape
Like newly cooked bread, muffins or cake

Pleased with her efforts she did a second
And soon ideas manifested and beckoned
What she had completed friends wanted to see
Her talent was being unlocked with a new found key

"Really good" and "excellent" were comments made
Perhaps a small collection was in the making to be displayed
And so, it had begun; a new talent found
Creating depth and meaning without a sound

And more paintings came like clouds in the sky
Perhaps a portfolio for people to buy
A talent had been discovered buried beneath
Now brought out from deep underneath

And with paintings ready for all to view
The only thing left is for me to say; thank you
For putting paint to paper to discover something new
You inspire me to never just "make do"

The Homeless Man

Evening came; too early, too dark
I still needed to get to the park
My dog barked, he needed walking
Off the phone, I must stop talking

We were ready; hat, gloves and all
And opened the door, outside into fall
Leaves were turning; yellow, golden and red
A silence prevailed, it had to be said

Walking swiftly, all warm and cosy
I looked through windows inquisitive and nosey
And then a dark shadow took my eye
Approaching slowly did I hear a faint sigh?

A couple more steps, I moved closer
Focussing down under the poster
Amongst the rubbish and a beer can
There I could see, laying a man

I couldn't believe this was really his bed
Nothing moved, not an arm nor leg
"Hello, hello" was what I said
Was he asleep, was he dead?

His trousers dirty, his jacket torn
He lay there still, grey and forlorn
His matted beard and untidy hair
All I could do was stand and stare

What was his age, what was his name?
Then I thought, was he lame?
Should I leave, should I stay?
I knelt down as if to pray

I didn't know him but all the same
Leaving him there felt quite strange
Was he hungry, was he in pain?
No change had I as I looked in vain

Silence stopped, my dog gave a bark
I decided, I really must get to the park
Then come back and look again
Would he be exactly the same?

On my return he was still there
Laying peacefully in the night air
I made a decision; wrote out my number
With note in his hand, I left him in slumber

Today is going to be a boring day

Today is going to be a boring day
There's nothing much to do
I look out of the window
But there really isn't a view

So I lay on the bed
Thinking why is it boring
I yawn a bit and then some more
And soon I'm all but snoring

Today is going to be a boring day
There's nothing much to think
If I had some dirty cutlery or plates
I could wash them in the sink

So I go downstairs with despair
Thinking perhaps it could be better there
But alas it's just as boring
There's only a table and one chair

Today is a boring one
The day ticks on and on
They say time is precious
But today feels like a con

Eventually it is dark
The sun and sky are gone
It's certainly been a boring day
Tomorrow I will ring my friend John!

The Milk Bottle

Early morning here comes the van
Milk bottles rattling and a milkman

One pint delivered I'm sitting there still
Not doing anything; waiting for the thrill

And then a blue tit flies over the top
Milk available? I think not

But the bird flies close, hovers and flutters
Mmm I want milk, the goodness it mutters

And then the beak pierces my top
It's nice and thick, it's almost a clot

Soon breakfast is finished, off it flies
That was yummy it shouts and cries

And then the door opens and hands come down
I'm picked up by someone with a frown

Transported to the kitchen and into the fridge
I sit on the shelf like a mountain ridge

It's very cold and full to the brim
Everything looks tasty there's nothing grim

Finally, it's my time to take centre stage
I'm poured out over cereal like a waterfall with rage

And then I'm finished put back inside
I wait for my next task to flow again like a tide

The Passing

A man who had lived in South America and Dover
His life was ending, it was nearly over

He lay there still, breaths slow and shallow
His skin depleted of colour and increasingly sallow

But not alone and surrounded by family at his side
It was his time; he was ready to glide

His physical body a vehicle for this life
Not needed for his soul to meet again his wife

The memories held strong, never to be forgotten
As clear as fields of white floating cotton

Transcending from one world to the next
It was peaceful and loving, simplicity at its best

And then he was gone; in the physical world no more
He had entered a world of pure light at its core

The world of souls had opened its door
And somewhere else a new baby was once more

Strength Within

I lay here motionless day by day
I reflect, I think and I suppose I pray

Not in a religious way, more spiritual, looking for the light
At least something to help relieve me of my plight

Time and time again; where is the answer, where is the path?
I want to feel warm and peaceful like you do after a hot bath

What I see and feel is black and white and maybe some grey
But I know the colours of the world are there, like lights on Broadway

I want to hear and feel, I want to see
Confidence, happiness and motivated to be

The person I know I was, the person I want back
He is hidden without nourishment or a savoury snack

For a moment I want to open the window and feel the air
The wind enters and, in the room, it is everywhere

I look at the window, there is a world out there
I want to be part of it, I want to be able to share

The good things for definite but maybe even some bad
Laying here still and motionless I must be mad

Yes, hunger and pain abound the world
And here I am, a body and mind all curled

But I know the night stars continuously shine
The sun stands proud, warm rays enjoyed and it is fine

A trickle of strength in the odd breath I take
Too much pain, anguish, self-loathing and hate

Can I turn the clock back, change the wheel?
My desire to be better I cannot conceal

It's time I looked forward and was good to me
To be buzzing, flying like a carefree summer bee

Yes, I can learn how to survive
And yes, I want to know why I'm alive

To love life and have a healthy smile
It won't be easy, it will take a while

But something tells me I'm ready; let the battle to strength begin
I know its inside; my body, my soul, my spirit, it's there within

I will harness its power like the wind, water and sun
The journey of my strength within has now begun

What is Joy?

Perhaps it's the sunshine after the rain
Shining down on the window pane
Or is it the river with a never ending flow
Or the winds of summer warmth we all want to blow

Is it lying in bed on a cold frosty morning?
Or the tip of the sun setting and dawning
Maybe its togetherness sharing the chores
Or your dog begging and giving you its paws

Maybe it's just doing stuff all things great
Or stoking the hot cinders in the grate
Could it be a huge loving smile?
Looking big, wider than a mile

Is it picking me up when I feel down?
Or making me happy by acting the clown
Perhaps it's receiving a surprise present
Or a warm glowing moon in its crescent

Is it knowing what the other is thinking?
Or wiping my tears when I am blinking
Perhaps it's when I feel elated
And so grateful I was created

Maybe it's appreciation of my favourite chocolate tart
The warm fuzzy feeling in my heart
But whatever it is it is something to treasure
Because what it gives is heaps of pleasure

The Heatwave

A few days over thirty
The air polluted stale and dirty
Thermal low or thundery depression
The weatherman says it will make an impression

They call it a Spanish plume on its way north
Soon over France and definitely on course
And then the clouds white to black
And as if by magic a sudden crack

The lightning first then the thunder
This is no time to blunder
The first raindrops hit the window pane
And then the storm – it's insane

Mobiles filming the lightning and rain
It's only weather but all the same
It's like a bath with no soap
As if there is not much hope

Flash floods and cars pulling over
What's needed is a four leaved clover
And then just like that the rain begins to stop
We can relax, Britain isn't about to pop

The cleaner air sweeps in like a brush
And the sky – well more like a blueberry crush
Temperatures down to nearer normal
And well we are back to being formal

At least until the next heatwave

Our Village of Writtle

Our village of Writtle is loved so dearly
Just walk around, you can see why clearly
Close to Chelmsford our neighbouring city
Writtle is small, compact and amazingly pretty

At the original centre the village green
It's not to be missed, it must be seen
Complete with pond, benches and ducks
Retained is character; there are no Starbucks

The weeping willows stand so proud
You will very rarely see a crowd
But residents all say hello and smile
Often chatting for more than a while

Surrounded by ancient cottages and aged architecture
Or attend the university college for a well-informed lecture
Wander around; there is plenty to look at
The very observant may spot the hanging cricket bat

Or the met office station with its Stephenson Screen
And when you are hungry there is plenty of cuisine
Indian or Italian are both on the menus
Two restaurants we have, are both superb venues

As well as cafes and pubs such as the Rose and Crown
A beer or two you can quietly down
And standing tall the church; a place to think and reflect
A hub of activity its presence perfect

A friendly place with real community
Writtle prides itself on its sense of unity

Angel in Disguise

You are an angel in disguise
Full of help, intelligence and very wise

Through the good times and the bad
You are there never ever sad

With unconditional love and warmth, a plenty
Your heart full and never empty

With one wish only it would definitely be
To give you as much as you've given me

And whilst I've given you some cloudy days
You've been my sunshine in so many ways

Through trials and tribulations there you stood
You gave me your love whenever you could

Thank you so much, for being there
Ensuring I remember you always care

My gratitude and thanks have no limit
Like a clock ticking by a second and a minute

Winter snow

Outside the wind blows so cold
Frozen pipe weather, if be told
Snowflakes fall and start to settle
Swirling gently like a petal

The white stuff continues on its flight
Downwards to earth turning it white
First to be covered is the grass
And then car roofs as they pass

Soon the pavements and the roads
This is no weather for frogs and toads
Minus 7 overnight
Winter is here its grip so tight

And now it's morning
The pure white blanket is calling
I go walking in the crisp bright snow
Watching for snow covered branches with a robin or a crow

The icy layer underfoot goes crunch
The cold on my face has such a punch
As if the snow whispers in my ear
Shhh, quiet and stillness is so clear

With children sledging and throwing snowballs
It is lunchtime, hot soup and bread calls
The quiet silent noise of falling snow
Almost timeless as clocks move seemingly more slow

Penguins

We are penguins clothed black and white
Our waddle and walk an adorable sight

Slipping and sliding on the ice and snow
The freezing water not far below

We may not fly but we can swim
Catching fish to eat, full to the brim

Surviving the harsh winter, the bitter gales
Gliding over the ice like a yacht with sails

But the Antarctic winds blow so strong
Making snow horizontal; harsh for too long

And to keep us warm we huddle together
Waiting for a lull in the bleak, bad weather

And when our babies are born and hatched
Our joy and happiness cannot be matched

We have lots of fun, on our chest
Diving into water at our best

And when we've finished feathers wet and plump
A leap in the air, we take a jump

Back on the ice with our spot to keep
We close our eyes and are off to sleep

What is love?

Love; the meaning how to describe
It's not a recipe we can prescribe

Is it the fuzzy feeling in your heart?
Or when you know it's being torn apart

Is it hot chocolate with marshmallow and cream?
Or the happy ending in our dream

The friend standing by you when things get tough
Or the hot soup you're given when feeling rough

Staying and listening and doing what's great
Even if doing so makes you late

Perhaps it's a simultaneous sinking when the other is down
Or the longing to help others remove their inner frown

Happy Easter to everyone

With chocolate bunnies and chocolate eggs
Why is there hatred in the world, the question begs

Let's all do our bit and reduce the pain
After all we are all humans and really just the same

All wanting happiness, health and love
So, release in your mind; a beautiful dove

Happy Easter

Blue and Purple

Spring has arrived, the sun grows stronger
Nights shorten and days get longer
With dewy moisture on the meadow glade
Under the trees is a dappled shade

And covering the floor like a glistening honey glaze
I see a mixture of blue and purple haze
Warm sunshine streaming down from above
We enter the trees with caution and love

The bluebells, individual, each standing proud
Pulling together to form one vast crowd
So many simple elements to each little flower
Yet they grow there strong with such unique power

And like an army ready and waiting
A beautiful scene they are creating
Every step taken with thought in my mind
The carpet of blue I want to be kind

Like sapphires shining in dazzling light
The bluebells in their hundreds content and bright
Each flower moving gently in the breeze
With fluttering butterflies and buzzing bees

It is May and it is now time
For the bluebell to be centre stage and shine

Robin arrives

Summer sun moves to Autumn leaves
Swallows gathering under the eaves
Flowers die back and colours fade
And more and more garden in the shade
The smiles of warm sunny days now long gone
The central heating, we want fully turned on

And with vegetables picked for eating and freezing
The first signs of cold and we are sneezing
An array of berries ripen from red to black
And as if by magic the robin is back
Perched on a twig or a spade's wooden handle
It brightens up the garden like a flame to a candle

Hello Robin "how do you do"
We love you so much, if only you knew
Your splash of colour a beautiful display
Especially welcome on a dark dank day
It's lovely to see and hear you sing
Joy to the heart you always bring

And there you are, day after day
Eating worms and insects in our garden café
You provide us plenty of winter joy
Like happiness to a child with a new toy
And as we dig in the compost and earth
You sit there not knowing how much you are worth

And drink you do at the water filled bath
Or hopping merrily along the stone path
And when it snows your red breast glows
In all its glory like a winter rose
You're a sparkle in the garden like a ruby treasured
Our love for you is huge, it cannot be measured

Our little frog

A little frog sits by the pond
Under the fern's hanging frond
He's not very big, quite small in fact
Skin all wet and never cracked

He looks smooth and slimy, brownish green
He is new to the garden, where has he been?
And sitting there he croaks so loud
Watching us, beady eyed as if he is proud

And so, we decided to give him a name
He is ours after all, or so we claim
Named him Tom, it's simple to say
Often around not far does he stray

With eyes moving this way and then the other
It's possible he could be a father or a mother
We don't really know, it's hard to tell
Whether the pond is his house or hotel

He looks happy to sit there, swim or float
On a lily pad, his own personal boat
And as evening comes, is he yawning?
See you tomorrow, early, in the morning

Social Media; good or bad?

Is Social media here to stay?
Or should we really keep it at bay

People who've never met, following what we do
Is it at all real or even true?

Should we believe all we see
Probably not; a complete life it cannot be

Feeling lonely, worried, anxious or lost
The virtual world, there for you but at what cost

And before we knew it, a nation of comparing
Photos, number of likes; a screen we keep on staring

Pictures of breakfasts or wine glasses at lunch
Or a mixture of both – it's usually called brunch

And yes, it can be nice to see a countryside scene
Or maybe where real friends have visited and been

But from Facebook to Instagram and tic toc too
Do we really understand or have a clue?

Notifications, a ring, a vibrate, a text
Our minds wander; what comes next?

A virtual world, it's quite surreal
So much time spent that's just not real

We know it's available but are we addicted
Good or bad we become conflicted

How much screen time seems never enough
But really much is nonsense and well, just stuff

With limited depth and minimal meaning
If you think it's good maybe you are dreaming

We know already it affects our health
For many it's depleting our emotional wealth

Yet we continue more and can't switch off
It's getting worse than an irritating cough

For that we can take medication or a drug
But for this we need to completely unplug

And is what we see true reflections of life
Or more like cutting out segments like cake with a knife

So why is it popular, why is it there?
The money and profit, businesses only care

Algorithms in the background monitor our moves
Watching and managing us, looking for clues

What are our interests, what adverts can they send?
We are bombarded, are they a real friend

The question we must ask is; what does it do?
Who does it help, the many or the few?

Taking us away from reality and friends
It's doubtful it does anything to actually cleanse

So, put down that phone or close the screen
And notice what's around you and where you have been

Sock mystery

Laundry done, time to take stock
And as usual I find a leftover sock

The other missing; where is it hiding?
The pair together so often deciding

Two does work, but one is no good
Like a newly created fire with no wood

It seems to happen more than a lot
Hard to understand like a murder mystery plot

So, they are kept in the bottom drawer
First, just one then two and then more

Yes, I could chuck them but there is a catch
If the other turns up there won't be a match

So, I keep them neatly year after year
Waiting for the other to eventually appear

But the drawer fills up; I can't ignore
It's full to bursting and can take no more

So, it's time to act and make a stand
The single socks are in my hand

The decision is made, they must go
And finally, I have found the courage to throw

Rainbow

With sunshine and raindrops mixing and falling
Mother nature may come knocking and calling

Not lasting forever so take it all in
A rainbow in the sky appears within

An arc of red, orange, yellow and green
There are seven colours in total to be seen

The others are indigo, violet and blue
All neatly arranged like people in a queue

And the mystery remains, we never really get nearer
Less distance doesn't help or make it clearer

It is magical for my eyes to behold and see
For all of us, but especially me

To brighten my day and make me smile
It won't last long; be gone in a while

Some say it's a gift or present from above
Like the heavenly purity of a white flying dove

And find that gold we never can
It doesn't exist like the gingerbread man

And so, fades that arc deep colours no more
The sky now becomes, what it was before

So much to me

My head feels like it's in an explosion
It's brimming over with lots of emotion
You gave so much love and so much thought
And you never, ever, denied any support
You were my darkness and my light
My left and my right

My past, present and future
A body cut, needing a suture
We went together like bread and butter
Never a crossed word, at most a mutter
And the strength and power of our devotion
Leaves my heart in such a commotion

You were my tulips from Amsterdam
My pearl treasured; in a clam
The icing spread on my wedding cake
The golden sunrise at every daybreak
My waves on a beach gently lapping
A birthday present with extra wrapping

My friend, my confidant, my truly ever
Did we argue, not really, never?
And you a rainbow in the storm
A beautiful crocus from a hibernating corm
And like a snowflake drifting gently down
You smiled so much; never a frown

And whilst your physical body is no more
You will, forever, remain at my core
Always you are deep in my heart
Our souls together will never be apart
I love you too much, I just can't bear
But now you have taken the steps up heaven's stair

A spiritual gift

A little gift from me to you
To celebrate Christmas through and through
My sister Karen, very special and loved so dearly
A beautiful relationship we have so clearly

Without you life would be less good
Like Christmas Day without traditional "pud"
So, I hope you like my spiritual present
Like a shining moon with its silver crescent

Imperial Jasper; powerful healer of the heart
Will keep us close and never apart
And like other Jaspers it is a protective stone
Helping to make sure we are never alone

Helping us to relax, it has strong healing
It's a gem of a stone, very appealing
Whereas Topaz crystal is transparent and pure
Releasing stress, it acts as a cure

To balance, soothe and cleanse emotions
It's like calming the waves on nature's oceans
In a spiritual sense it brings peace and love
Fitting you like a hand to a glove

One Single Poem

One single poem was read aloud
In the market square to a crowd
On a Sunday every week
Whether sunny and warm or cold and bleak

At exactly 10 the bells would ring
And many people they would bring
Men and woman and children too
Would gather there ready, right on cue

Some people thought and some reflected
New friendships developed; community connected
A range of poems had always been read
A highlight for some, they rushed out of bed

The firsts words were spoken loud and clear
Would they be funny or bring a tear?
Some were short and to the point
Others were longer and became sort of joint

Side stalls offering coffee and tea
On Sunday mornings a drink was free
And listen with interest and enthusiasm too
Every week poems different and new

And when the poems were at an end
The people applauded sometimes with a new friend
No money was collected it wasn't needed
The message of community and support always seeded

And so, the people dispersed and went on their way
To do whatever they wanted on this special day

Old and Grey

I may be old and may be grey
But I still have lots of things to say
If you care to listen you might learn
Knowledge and respect you may earn
When I was young, we made do
Often second hand and nothing new

Clothes with holes were always patched up
You drank every last drop in your cup
If it was cold, we put on another layer
We made games fun, had no record player
And at mealtimes we ate what was given
Rarely full but it kept us energetic and driven

Gardens were used for growing food
Even if tired and we weren't in the mood
Every week and day organised with chores
No handy massive out of town stores
And although my skin may be wrinkled and sag
I know for sure we can brag

We looked after each other, knew everyone in the street
Provided help and support when needed, whether snow or sleet
But today technology so fast I can't keep up
I like to see family and friends close up
And yes, I may seem grumpy and out of touch
Seemingly needing a wooden stick as a crutch

But I have lived through good times and bad
Steady and strong and sometimes got mad
But ignore me at your peril, I won't be walked over
If lucky you will see me like a four-leaf clover

Train Delay – again

It's 7am on a cold January morning
Dark and wet and I'm still yawning
I arrive to see the crowds of people
Congregating like a church under its steeple

The train delayed, yet again
This is ridiculous, a complete pain
With leaves or snow or tracks too hot
Out network of trains is going to pot

Twenty minutes pass, we move slightly ahead
With tiny steps we can only tread
Finally the stairs and up we flow
And then on the platform we get ready to go

Finally standing with the masses
Men and women, lads and lasses
The train in the distance we move into position
Our one final, focussed and important mission

Get on the train, stand or sit
My energy sinking, I can admit
Off we move, slowly at first
And then it jolts as if it is cursed

People pressed together with raincoats wet
Someone's eating breakfast, a bacon baguette
Windows steaming up with nothing to see
Resting on the seat end with my knee

Mobiles ring, books and papers rustle
So many mornings start with hustle and bustle
Silence prevails, nobody speaks
The carriage being old subtly creaks

10 minutes have past and we grind to a halt
Driver speaks - "signal failure it's not my fault"
People huff and puff and glance at each other
The odd groan, the odd mutter

Eventually we have movement of the train
The windows still wet with heavy rain
Finally, late, the station I arrive
Yet another journey I survive

Everyone files out like ants to a nest
Faces fraught; too many looking stressed
So, leaving the office seven hours have past
Still wet and windy I walk fast

Enter the mainline station, I am here
But listen to the speakers I overhear
"Due to leaves on the line trains are delayed"
I tense up, anger rises, I feel betrayed

The annual season ticket, it's so expensive
For such a bad service is incomprehensive
So, I join the crowds of people once more
Déjà vu I've been here before!

Cup of Tea

The drink of the British
The good old cup of tea

A herb not a spice
So many agree a cuppa is nice

Originally from China we think it is ours
Well, we all know we can drink it for hours

Whenever a crisis, a problem or two
We turn on the kettle to make a hot brew

Let's make a cup of tea as if that makes things better
Like receiving a you've won a prize or money letter

Whether in a cup and saucer or just a mug
Some of us could drink it by the jug

On its own or with a biscuit or two
From an elderly lady to a builder's crew

In olden days the grouts remained
Even after the tea had been strained

Full of flavour and goodness too
We love our cuppa, our traditional brew

For some it's milk and a dip of the bag
For others it dark, solid and a tannin to brag

It's hot, refreshing and easy to make
Just dip in the bag for a welcome break

Morning lunch or evening time
Having several is never a crime

But it's not just Yorkshire, Red Label or PG Tips
We have Camomile or Dar jeeling or fruits without pips

Once used some go straight in the bin
Others are collected in a jar or a tin

And for those being green the compost heap
The remaining goodness to breakdown and keep

But however, you drink your cup of tea
Reward yourself with one, two or three

Christmas

Christmas has come, it's finally here
In all its glory and festive cheer
Decorate the tree for all to see
"Can we open a gift" the children plea

Presents underneath carefully wrapped
After the Queens speech we rested and napped
The smell of Christmas is better than fine
With mixed fruits, cinnamon or warm mulled wine

And if you can, fire burning logs
A warm, snoozy place for so many dogs
But Christmas sentiment is not just one day
Supporting, loving and caring should not be put away

Bows and ribbons tied neatly and tight
Candles and lanterns offer flickering light
And when the turkey is ready to be carved
Our mouths watering as if we had been starved

Crackers pulled and hats on our heads
Laughter and joy develops and spreads
And you never know with your Christmas "pud"
You may find a sixpence if you have been good

And party games old and new
Give so much enjoyment it is true
But remember some people are single and alone
No children to see, or families flown

Christmas carols we love to hear
Santa Claus with his sleigh and several reindeer
And Christmas cards hang from wall to ceiling
Each picture and message so very appealing

And if you are lucky with the mistletoe
You may get a kiss standing there below
It's a time for mince pies and brandy butter
Although not everyone likes them; yuk they mutter

But when Christmas is over, decorations packed away
For some it has been a time too sad and grey
And with the new year Spring will seed
So be caring and kind and do a good deed

Being Mum

Can you clear the floor and clothes away?
I can't stand seeing it another day
The bedroom again is full of clutter
"Oh ok" they growl or mutter

And returning from school you ask "how was your day?"
"Fine", no detail they just about say
And when it's time you dish out the dinner
They look at it as if you are a sinner

I don't like this and I don't like that
You feel like you're treated like a doormat
When they were a baby it was broken sleep, cleaning and feeding
And so often one book after another reading

You rocked them to sleep and gave them food
They appreciated you then – were never rude
As they got older, they expected more
Sometimes stressing you to the core

If it wasn't one thing, two things or another
Pulled in different directions; you were a mother
You lent them a fiver and became their taxi driver
But as are all mums you remained a survivor

You loved them lots and very dearly
But drive you mad they could clearly
And give them confidence and mop their tears
You helped them with their fears

Being a mum is often hard
Nobody gave you a readymade instruction card
And is it worth it; yes of course
Your life and love, they are a central source

Happy 40th Birthday

Happy 40th Birthday in this very strange year
2020 has so far, been anything but clear
With the Covid 19 virus taking centre stage
All we want is to turn a new page

Still keeping safe and a lot of staying at home
We even remembered how to speak on the phone
And now your birthday at the easing of lockdown
It's not even worth just wandering into town

No cafes or restaurants open to eat
And if there were, probably queues to beat
In normal times we would be packing our cases
Now the best we can do is to tie our laces

A local walk or slightly further afield
For now, at last I don't need to shield
What to buy you has been so hard
We can't drink coffee in a medieval courtyard

Or fly to a warm beach with waters blue
So, from me to you, here is a clue
You can keep this for the future, it won't go out of date
You don't need to rush, it can certainly wait

Use at your discretion, the choice is yours
Maybe inside or even outdoors
But either way, I wanted to say
You're 40, have a Happy Birthday

Last Poem

So, my 50 poems you may have read
Whether on the sofa or in your bed

I hope you have enjoyed my 2020 collection
For this special book is a varied selection

Some may have made you laugh or just smile
Others brought back memories for a long or short while

Perhaps you took a few minutes to reread and reflect
Thoughts and memories to cherish and collect

But in a world fast changing and very diverse
It is a life to live and not to rehearse

Understanding and compassion wins every time
Negativity and hate are a wasteful crime

So, remember the simplest actions can help the most
Cementing solid foundations like a fence needs a post

And if I can ask you one thing or maybe two
Always try and see a cloudy sky as sunny and blue

A Message from Tim

I hope you have enjoyed reading "A Pocketful of Poems".

A number of the poems are based on my own personal experiences and interactions as well as aspects of life which are important or have made a difference. The uniqueness and challenges of 2020 have sometimes influenced my writing.

I am sure individual poems will resonate with different people such as those who visit the gym or have dogs.

Perhaps some will have made you smile or reflect about your own life or experiences. Maybe thinking about what is important in life or makes a difference.

But whether you have smiled or reflected or just enjoyed reading the poems please feel free to lend the book to others to enjoy.

Printed in Great Britain
by Amazon

54123911R00037